Step-by-Step to a Classic
FIREPLACE MANTEL

Steve Penberthy
with Gary Jones

Text written with
and photography by
Douglas Congdon-Martin

A complete
guide to building
a classic fireplace
mantel from
stock materials

Schiffer Publishing Ltd
77 Lower Valley Road, Atglen, PA 19310

Contents

Copyright © 1994 by
Stephen Penberthy
Library of Congress Catalog Number: 94-65609

Printed in China
ISBN: 0-88740-653-X

We are interested in hearing from authors
with book ideas on related topics.

Published by Schiffer Publishing Ltd.
77 Lower Valley Road
Atglen, PA 19310
Please write for a free catalog.
This book may be purchased from the publisher.
Please include $2.95 postage.
Try your bookstore first.

Introduction

If you've been thinking that your fireplace could use some dressing up, but you've given up on the idea because you think that a mantel is an expensive hand-crafted piece of furniture, then this book is for you. The assembly methods shown in this book will make it easy for you to build your classic fireplace mantel...at a price you can afford!

The fireplace and fireplace mantel are always the focal point of a room. The mantel usually reflects the architecture of the house as well as the individual style of the occupant. The mantel's design and finish, whether hardwood or softwood, painted or stained, set the mood and establish the flavor of a room.

This book will help you build the fireplace mantel that best fits your home. Although I've chosen to build our most popular mantel, the construction methods are the same for an almost endless variety of styles.

Probably the first question people have, after they see our mantels, is "How much will it cost?" We all know that hardwood is expensive, as are the tools necessary to work with it. The cost of this mantel is kept down by not using solid hardwood for the front piece and legs. Instead you will use hardwood faced plywood. Hardwood plywood is more expensive than softwood plywood. But it's quite a bit less expensive than hardwood lumber. It is also easier to "mill" with the kind of tools we have around the house.

Stock moldings are used to finish off the mantel. There are hundreds of patterns of these moldings available. Because the milling has already been done, the only tools necessary are saws to cut-to-length and miter them.

If you are in a part of the country where moldings aren't available or if you have any questions or comment about the book, please send me a self addressed stamped envelope, and I will be glad to help you find a nearby source of materials.

Steve Penberthy
212 N.E. Sixth Avenue
Portland, OR 97232

The Multnomah Mantel

Suggested Tools and Supplies

One from each catagory:

1. Table saw with tilting arbor (sled for cross-cutting helpful)
2. A. Miter box
   or B. Electric miter saw
   or C. Sliding compound miter saw
3. A. Biscuit joiner
   or B. Drill motor and doweling jig with 3/8" brad point bit
4. A. Hammer and nail set
   or B. Finish nail gun or staple gun with 1-1/4" fasteners
5. A. Hammer, 1-1/4" finish nails, and drill with 3/64" bit to pilot holes
   or B. Pin nailer for attaching mouldings

6. 5 foot bar or pipe clamps (2 or more)
7. 12" bar clamps (2 or more)
8. 100 grit sandpaper (2 sheets minimum)
9. 150 grit sandpaper (2 sheets minimum)
10. 220 grit sandpaper (2 sheets minimum)
11. 400 grit sandpaper (2 sheets minimum)
12. 600 grit sandpaper (2 sheets minimum)
13. A. Sanding block
    or B. Electric sander
14. Tack Cloth
15. Wood filler for miters and joints
16. Wood glue
17. Clear wood finish
18. Combination square

Parts List

3/4" Red Oak plywood*	1 sheet	O020 Bead Board	10'
8/4 Red Oak -2 pieces	7" wide, 5" long	O6007 fillet (or mantel open trim)	13'
O745 mantel moulding	10'	3/8" x 2" fluted dowel pins**	4
O724 base cap	14'		
O610 crown moulding	10'		

*Additional plywood may be necessary for over-size mantels
** Biscuits may be substituted

Moulding Profiles

O-724
Base Cap
3/4" x 1-1/8"

O-745
Mantel mould
11/16" x 1-1/2"

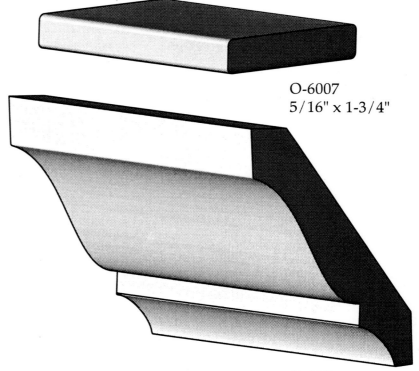

O-6007
5/16" x 1-3/4"

O-610
11/16" x 3-7/16"

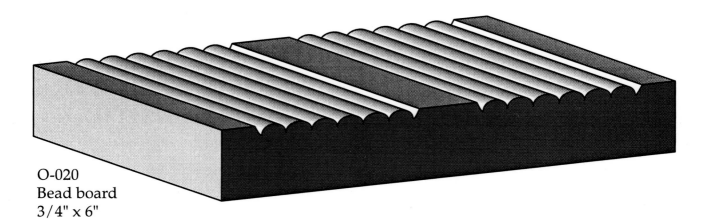

O-020
Bead board
3/4" x 6"

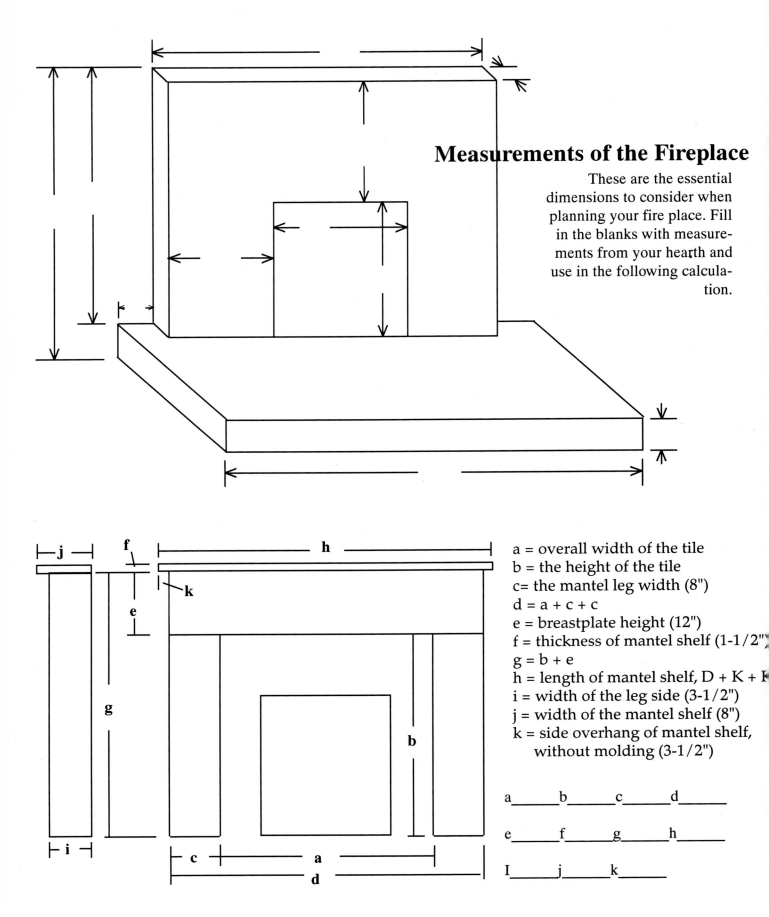

Measurements of the Fireplace

These are the essential dimensions to consider when planning your fire place. Fill in the blanks with measurements from your hearth and use in the following calculation.

a = overall width of the tile
b = the height of the tile
c= the mantel leg width (8")
d = a + c + c
e = breastplate height (12")
f = thickness of mantel shelf (1-1/2")
g = b + e
h = length of mantel shelf, D + K + K
i = width of the leg side (3-1/2")
j = width of the mantel shelf (8")
k = side overhang of mantel shelf, without molding (3-1/2")

a_____ b_____ c_____ d_____

e_____ f_____ g_____ h_____

I_____ j_____ k_____

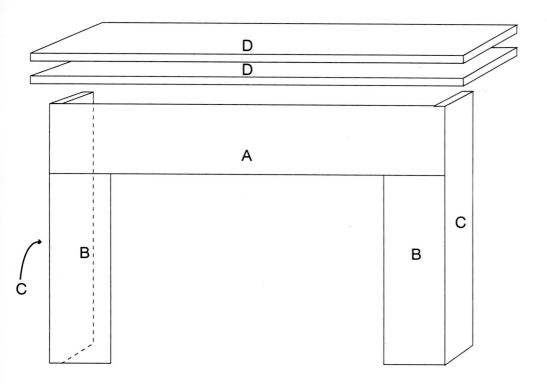

The Mantel Parts and the Plywood Layout

BREASTPLATE: A = width e x length d
LEG FACE B = width c x length b
LEG SIDE C = width i x length g
MANTEL SHELF D = width j x length h
CROWN STEP E = 1" x length d
   (not shown)

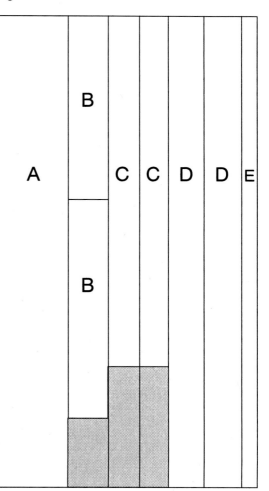

Building the Mantel

Begin by cutting the plywood into strips. Set the guide to the appropriate width and run the plywood through. This is 3/4" red oak, A-1 plywood. The first strip to cut is 12" wide for the breast plate.

Next cut two pieces 8" wide which will be used for the mantel shelf.

The leg face will be 8" wide, but rough cut it at 8-1/4" so you can come back and bevel one edge at a 45 degree angle. Cut both leg faces from the same piece of plywood

The sides of the legs will finish at 3-1/2", but cut them at 3-3/4" because they, too, will be beveled. You need two pieces, so repeat this step.

Next we need a 1" wide extender to go under the crown molding. The crown molding projects out from the face on this particular style of mantel.

Cut the breast plate using on the table saw using a sled jig. This allows a mitered cut of 45 degrees at each end. A sled jig makes this cut much easier. With the face side up it is much easier to see the mark. The long dimension of this piece is 76".

With the saw set at 45 degrees, run the leg face and sides back through the blade to bevel one side. This time the saw guide should be set at exactly 8" for the face and 3 1/2" for the sides, and the pieces will run through face down. (Our saw tilts to the right to allow for this. If your tilts to the left, cut with the legs face up and adjust the fence 3/4" closer to compensate.)

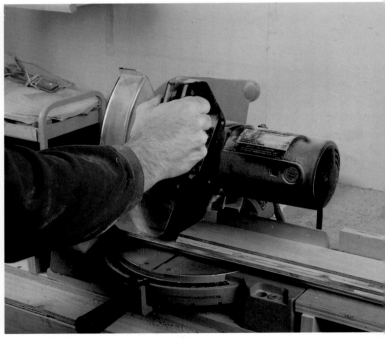

Cut off the pieces to length. I am using a chop saw, but you could do it on the sled or with a hand miter box. The two top pieces are at 83", the leg sides are 52", the leg faces are 40". When two pieces, like the leg sides, are the same length, I align them face to face and cut them together. The crown extender piece will be cut to length later, to ensure a perfect fit.

The easiest way to join the leg face to the breast plate is with a biscuit joiner. Lay the pieces face down on the work bench. Align them and make marks for position at the joint of the breast and leg plates. These should be about 2" in from the sides of the leg. Two biscuits will do it.

and the breast plate in the same way.

Apply glue to the mortises of the leg face.

Match the guide line of the biscuit joiner with the marks you made and cut the mortise for the biscuit. Do the leg...

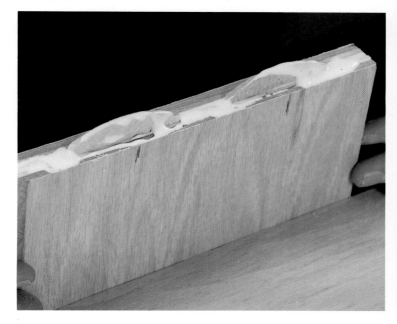

Glue the biscuits. I want enough glue to ensure a strong joint, but I try to keep most of it toward the back of the biscuit to keep it from oozing out on the front of my mantel piece. By putting enough glue on at this time, I don't have to go to the trouble of putting glue in the mortises of the breast plate.

Join the leg face to the breast plate, being sure the beveled edges line up. There should be some ooze on the back, and very little on the front. For the little that does come out in the front, it might be a good idea to put plastic between the mantel and your workbench.

With the leg in a vise, align the reference line of the doweling jig with the reference line on the leg face. Tighten it in place.

Clamp the leg face and breast plate together. The clamp should be snug, but not tight enough to bow the work. Leave them in the clap long enough to dry.

An alternative way to join the leg to the breast plate is by doweling. It is a little harder to do. You begin in the same way, by aligning the leg face with the breast plate and drawing reference marks. Again, two dowels are enough.

I use a 3/8" brad point bit to drill the hole for the dowel deep. The point keeps it from walking as you start the hole. Drill a little more than an inch into the board. Repeat at the second line. Drill all eight holes before glue and assembly.

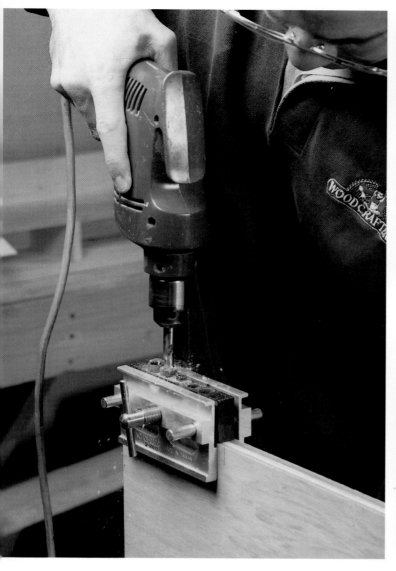

Insert them in the holes of the breast plate and drive them halfway down.

Repeat the process with the holes of the breast plate.

Apply glue to the holes of the leg face, making sure it is all around the hole and across the edge.

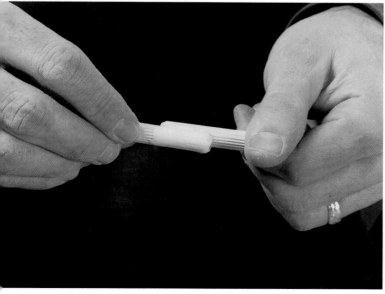

Apply and spread glue on the dowels.

Join the two pieces.

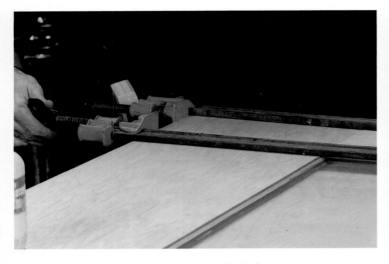

Clamps will pull them together the final distance.

Spread it with your finger to get a generous, even coating.

After the glue has set, situate the mantel so both ends of the side are overhanging the workbench.

Align the bottom and join. I do the bottom first because it has to be even so it will sit well on the floor. The top will be hidden by three inches of crown. I'm using a pneumatic nail gun, a 1" pinner.

Run a bead of glue up and down the beveled edge of the leg side.

Put another pin about four inches up from the first.

Move to the top, align the edge and place two more pins.

Drill four holes in the same spots as before, at the bottom, 4" from the bottom, at the top, and 4" from the top.

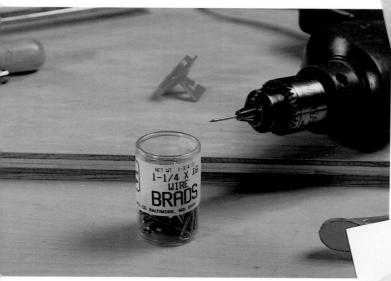

If you don't have a pneumatic tool you can use brads. You will need to make a pilot hole. I put one of the 1-1/4" brads I will be using in the chuck of my drill and use it to make the hole. I will go in about 3/4".

Hammer in the brads.

For this process you need to clamp the leg side firmly in place before drilling. Apply the glue to the joint and align the edge carefully.

Carefully turn the mantel completely over.

By turning the mantel over, gravity helps you align the edge while joining it together. The clamp brings the edges together. Drill the pilot holes for the brads.

With pneumatic nailer, I can use my free hand to align the edge as I nail it.

Drive home the brads.

While I hesitate to nail through the front, it sometimes is necessary. Here the glue set a little too long before nailing and tacking it from the front will help the alignment.

Ready for the top. Pick the best looking piece for the top.

Place the bottom piece good side down against the breast plate. Centering is based on the front corner of the breast plate, because there is no guarantee that the leg side is square. In this case there was a little under 3-1/2" overhang at each end.

Run glue on the inside of the line, except in the center where the breast plate sags some. There you come a little outside the line. Don't worry about glue oozing. It will be covered by molding.

Nail or staple the mantel top to the front corner of the breast plate.

Trace the bottom of the mantel on the underside of the top. This will give you a glue line.

The top shelf piece, laid on edge under the top, can act as a straight edge for getting rid of the sag in the breast plate. Lift the center of the breast plate to get rid of the sag and fasten from the top. If you are using nails, you may want to put a block under the breast plate to support it. Finish nailing across the top, only do not nail the lower part of the mantel shelf yet.

You will probably get a nail showing through. Don't worry, the crown will cover it.

Apply glue to the down side of the top shelf piece. Be sure to get around the edge, then apply a generous amount over the whole surface.

Check the square of the leg side, make any adjustments and nail it in place through the bottom shelf piece.

Stand it on its top. With 1-1/4" staples or nails tack the bottom to the top. If you keep the nails 1-1/2" from the edge, the crown molding will cover them.

Apply the top piece to the bottom shelf piece.

Nail behind the breast plate as well.

Align the corners and tack it down with one nail at each corner. This will hold it while you turn it over to nail from beneath.

Fill the two front joints between the breast plate and the leg faces. I use a latex solvent-free red oak filler. Work it into the crack with a putty knife.

I use 150 grit sandpaper on an orbital sander to clean up the fill. Be careful not to burn through the face of the veneer.

The crown molding is cut upside down and backwards, whether in a miter box or on a miter saw. The top molding has to flush with the bed of the table, and the back edge at the bottom has to be flush with the wall.

The 1" crown extender is aligned with one end of the breast plate and marked at the other. Cut it square.

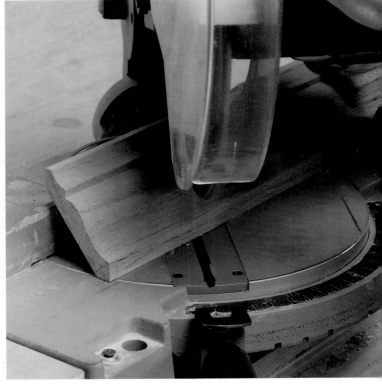

Cut one end of the crown molding at 45 degrees. If you are unsure of this cut, try it on a sample piece first.

Align the extender with the bottom edge of the beveled molding end...

I usually carry the line over the top so I can see it when I'm cutting.

and mark the molding at the other end of the extender.

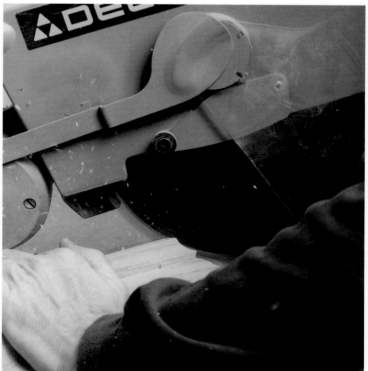

Change your cutting angle to the opposite direction, align the mark and cut it off. Remember to keep the edges of the molding flush with the table and wall of the saw fence.

Cut a miter on one of the return pieces to use for checking the angle of the crown molding. Leave the return long for now, to be sized later.

Run a bead of glue down the edge of the extender.

This simple check shows me I have a pretty good miter.

Nail the molding to the edge of the extender. If you are hand nailing it, clamp it first. Be certain the bottom of the molding is aligned with the face of the extender.

Also check the fit with the return.

Tack the moulding every 8-10 inches, enough to hold it in place, but not overly much. Check the alignment and adjust as you go.

Nail the molding into the extender using 1" nails or staples. The nails should not go into the breast plate.

After the molding is attached to the extender we attach the assembly to the breast plate, using an 1-1/2" staple or finish nail. Run a bead of glue down the edge of the extender.

Also run a bead along the back edge of the top of the crown molding.

Nail down one end.

Turn the molding assembly up and align it, using the return to help set it up correctly.

Cut the return for the other end and fit it.

24

Holding the return in place, nail the other end of the molding assembly. This gets the ends aligned correctly.

Now nail the length of the molding assembly to the face. Start at the center and work your way back out to the sides.

Switch back to the 1" nail or staple to nail the top edge. You want to put nails as close as necessary to keep the gap shut, probably about one every foot.

Hold the return in place and mark the point where it reaches the back side of the mantel.

Set the saw to zero degrees and cut the return off to the mark. I usually cut the returns a little long and sand them flush later.

A pinch dog will help hold the corner together while you nail it.

Apply glue to the three joining sides of the return.

Nail the return in place.

The result. This joint is probably the most important of the mantel. If there is a gap, you will never forgive yourself. It will look amateurish. If the joint is tight it is a source of pride. No one can do better! Work at it. Repeat at the other end.

Hold the face molding and the return in place, making sure the corner aligns. Mark the length of the return.

Miter the one end of the mantel shelf molding face and its return. The return, again, is for fitting, and should be cut long for now.

Cut the return just a little long, like we did on the crown molding.

Apply two lines of glue to the back of the return to hold it to the plywood.

Align one end of the face molding (a pinch dog will help it stay in position)...

With the face molding held in place, align the return and tack in place. The moldings stand about a paper's thickness above the surface of the mantel shelf; later we will go back and sand. When sanded they will be flush. The molding will also hang below the bottom of the shelf, but this is normal and is no need for concern. If it bothers you, you can always sand that edge flush too.

and mark the other end. Bring the line over the top so you can see when the molding is in the miter box.

Cut the miter at the end of the face molding and a longer-than-needed return piece.

Tack one end of the molding, check the other, and continue to work your way down the molding. Nail about every foot, through the thickest part of the molding, then come back and nail about every 18" through the thinner part. Remember to leave a paper's width above the mantel shelf surface.

Apply glue to the mitered end of the return that is already in place and to the edge of the mantel shelf. I apply two lines of glue to the edge, the lower one being far enough away from the bottom that the glue will not ooze out.

Mark the other return, cut it,

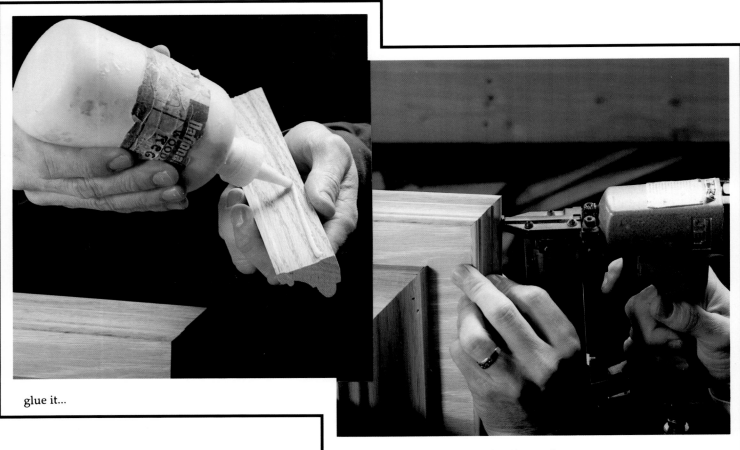

glue it...

carefully align it and nail it in place.

In measuring for the beaded panel molding that goes on the leg, mark the height of the foot on the leg face, which in this case is 5".

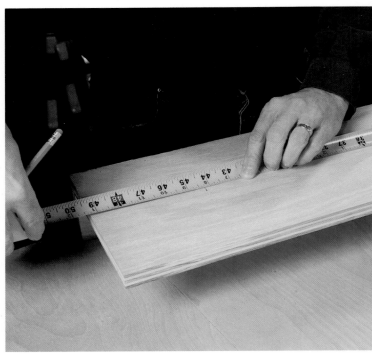

Measure down from the underside of the shelf to that point, in this case 44-1/4". Because of additional moldings there is some flexibility in this measurement, so don't fret over a quarter inch.

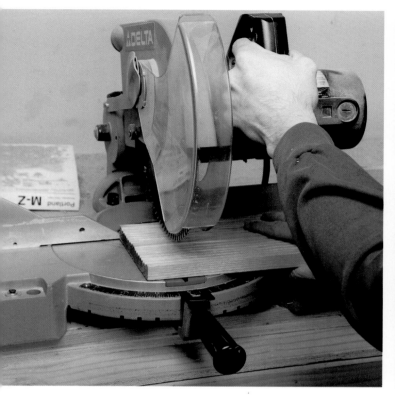

Cut the end of the molding to make sure it is square.

A seven inch piece of the beaded panel molding will be turned over to give a flat block at the top of the beaded panel. By using the end of the leg panels, you assure that the dimensionality and color of the wood will match. Mark and cut off seven inches from each of the panels.

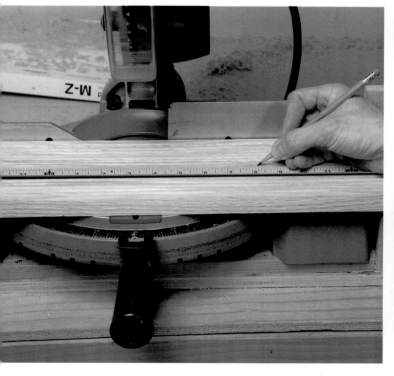

Mark and cut to length. Repeat for the other leg.

Use a combination square as a depth gauge to make sure the panel runs up the center of the leg. Measure in from one side...

and the other, making adjustments until it is correct. With the dimensions we are using for this mantel it should be about 1-1/4" in from each side, but minor adjustments will be necessary.

With the combination square already set from aligning the lower leg, you can use it to properly align the molding cap.

Run beads of glue on the molding cap. These three places are where the cap will come in contact with the face of the mantel.

Make sure the butt joint is as close as possible. Nothing will be covering this one.

Tack the cap in the four corners.

Make the top flush with the cap and use the combination square to set the bottom.

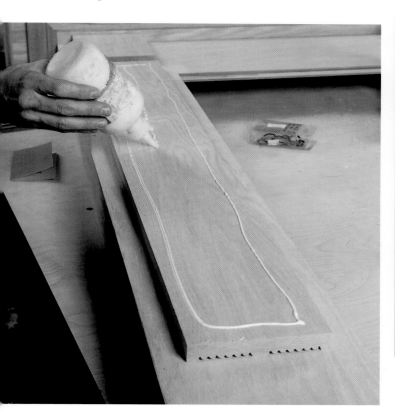

Apply glue to the back of the leg molding.

Tack it in place using six to eight nails.

This gap and any gap at the bottom of the leg molding is not important, since they will be covered by molding. Repeat at the other leg. The setting of the combination square should stay the same.

Center the piece in the same way you did the leg molding, using the combination square. We know it is roughly 1/2" but make minor adjustments so it is the same on both sides.

The feet are 7" wide and 5" high, cut from 1-1/2" stock. Mark and cut one at a time.

Glue generously, avoiding the edges.

34

Align it flush with the bottom

Nail from below, by overhanging the mantel. Repeat on the other leg.

Cut the face trim pieces. I begin with center piece that goes across the mantel face. Cut a 45 degree angle at one end.

Clamp in place so you can nail from the back. This is helpful because the foot is so thick.

Butt the mitered end in place, aligning it with the bottom edge of the molding cap.

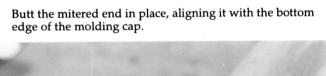

Align the other end with the molding cap and mark. Cut the miter.

Cut a miter for the inside return and mark the length.

Continue across the leg molding with another piece.

On the return, miter the back end, and measure at the front corner.

Miter the end of the next piece, hold it in place, and mark its length.

Check for fit.

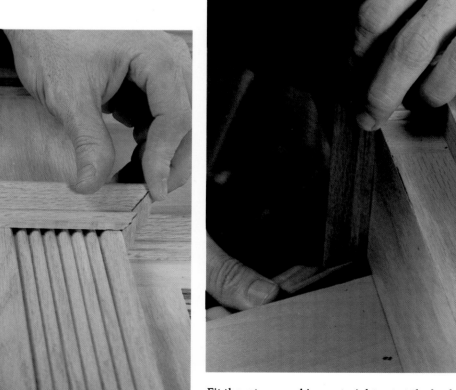

Fit the return, making a straight cut at the back to be flush with the edge of the mantel leg.

Repeat the process at the other end.

Run a bead of glue along the back of the center piece of molding.

Set the molding so it is pleasing to the eye, but be sure it covers the joint of the leg molding and cap. Set the combination square to the bottom edge. It is about 1-5/8" from the opening of the mantel.

Set one end using the square and nail it.

Work your way down the molding...

to the other end.

The inside return is so small we will just glue it in place. Glue the mitered surfaces and the back.

Apply glue to the trim that goes across the leg molding.

Use the combination square to set a straight line between the center molding and this piece.

Glue the next two pieces in place.

Nail in place.

Even though it is small, I risk putting one nail in this piece for strength. Any small crack will fill easily.

Glue the return and align it using the square. Nail in place.

Repeat at the other end.

Completed.

Mark the returns of the foot molding. The forward edge will be mitered, and the back will butt flush to the face of the leg, terminating there.

Make the mitered cuts here and on one end of the cross piece.

Cut the end and the return and check for fit with all three pieces.

Align the cross piece and mark.

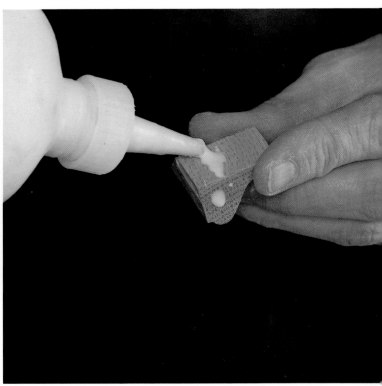

Apply glue to the pieces, gluing four sides of the returns.

Repeat at the other foot.

Hold in place and nail. I angle the nails into the foot, where l am more sure of making good contact.

Set all the nails. Nothing is more frustrated than to get to the sanding stage and discover you overlooked a nail.

The result.

Fill all the cracks and nail holes with water based latex filler. I start at the top of the shelf because it is a lot of surface area and by the time I finish the rest, it will be dry.

and the other to make sure I have the joint filled.

Fill the mitered edge joints This one along the leg is critical because it is one people will see. I work it from one side of the joint...

When the major edges are filled, work fill into the other joints...

Installing

and nail holes.

A nailset or other pointed tool can help you get into some of the tighter cracks.

Sanding on flat surfaces can be done with a sanding block or a orbital, random orbital or palm sander. Choose the one with which you are most comfortable. I use 100 grit paper for the rough sanding. I begin on the legs, then go to the front and, finally, the shelf.

Be careful not to sand through the veneer, or the glue and plywood beneath will show through like this.

Continue with the flat surface of the beaded panel.

With the flat surfaces done, I switch to 100 grit paper for hand sanding the contours of the molding. Get every nail hole, every joint, every pencil mark, and everywhere that glue has oozed out. The glue spots will not take stain so they must be sanded out.

A sanding stick helps me get into the corners.

This rough sanding will remove all the excess filler.

When the rough sanding is complete, go back over the mantel and find any voids.

Fill them...

and sand by hand with a 150 grit paper. Try to keep the sanding as uniform as you can. Areas that are sanded with different grits will take stain at a different rate and can appear splotchy.

Next we go to 220 grit paper. The finer you go with the sand paper, the smoother the finished product will be. For a super-smooth finish use 400 grit.

When you are satisfied with the smoothness of the legs and front, stand the mantel up and sand the shelf. This is 100 grit, and I'm taking the paper thin molding edge down to the surface of the shelf.

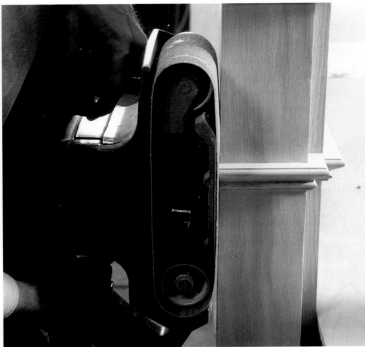

We left the returns of the molding a little long, so I hit them with a belt sander to flush them up. Be careful! A belt sander is very aggressive and will easily ruin your hard work.

Fill any cracks.

Hand sand the top with 150 grit paper...

A second sanding with 120 grit.

Followed by 220, then 400 grit for a smoother feeling finish.

Size the molding for the mantel opening. This is a spacer piece which will be ripped to bridge the gap between the edge of the mantel and the tile wall of the fireplace. There should be a bead of about 1/4" projecting beyond the front of the mantel and the back should be flush with the wall. While the ripping will be done later during installation, we size it now so we can stain and finish it to match the rest of the mantel. But first we will cut it to fit the opening. Begin with the cross piece. Cut a piece to the approximate length, and miter one end.

and mark the length. Cut it. Repeat on the other side.

Hold it in place and mark the other end.

Progressively sand the molding down to 220 grit, filling where necessary.

Miter one end of the side piece, hold it against the cross piece in place...

Clean up the dust with a tack cloth. Turn the cloth frequently to keep it from getting filled.

Follow the directions of the stain you choose. I like to use a cloth for application because it gives me more control. I drench the cloth and wring it out.

Let it set for 5-10 minutes and wipe it off with a clean cloth.

Work the stain into the fluting of the leg moldings.

Don't forget to do the trim.

Progress.

Do a final rub with the tack cloth.

Let the stain set for 8-12 hours then rub the surface one more time with a clean cloth.

Apply a clear, hard drying finish, following the directions of the particular finish you use.

Sand with 600 grit paper. Be careful of the edges, so you don't rub through the stain.

We follow the first coat with a wet sanding using 600 grit sandpaper.

Rub it down and let the finish dry.

We want the second coat to be as thin as possible. We use foam brushes and work the finish out until the brush is almost dry. Begin by applying a thin coat.

Before applying the second coat, sand lightly by hand with 600 grit paper. Use almost no pressure. Tack the piece clean.

Carry the finish up the piece until the brush is nearly dry.

Go back to the place where you first used the brush and go over it again. This will allow the brush to pick up some of the finish so you can carry it further. Be sure to flip the brush so you load both sides.

When a section is covered I go over it one more time without reloading the brush, taking all my strokes...

The brush is almost completely dry now, so I can use it to pull out these wet spots.

in the same direction.

Continue the same method over the whole mantel. Set it in a warm dry place to dry.

Before I leave a section I look for places where the finish is thick.

When the finish has dried overnight, lightly sand with 600 grit paper. At this stage we just work on the flat surfaces, and use a featherlight touch. We just want to take away the finest of bumps.

Tack the piece to remove any dust.

Measure 1 1/2" down from the top and make a mark.

Apply another thin coat. Work it out until the brush is dry.

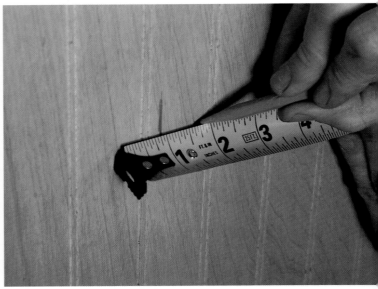

Measure in 3/4" from the side and mark.

When the finish has thoroughly dried, it is time to mount the mantel on the fireplace. Put the mantel against the wall where it will sit. Make sure it is centered over the opening. Trace a line around the outside.

Use a level to carry the line across the top at the mark...

and down the sides. These lines are for aligning the mounting blocks.

align on the wall and nail in place.

The mounting blocks are 2 x 4s. Run a bead of construction adhesive on one side...

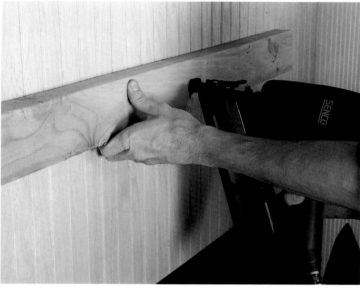

Do the same at the top.

Mount the mantle in place over the blocks and nail. You will come back and fill the nail holes.

The opening trim should fill the gap between the mantel and the tile. Nail the side piece in place first.

Then bend the middle piece to it fits between them.

Nail in place, and fill all the nail holes and touch up the finish.

The final product.

The Gallery